SandCastle™ Primeros Sonidos

Valeria y Víctor

Cathy Camarena, M.Ed., and Gloria B. Ruff, M.Ed.

Consulting Editors
Lourdes Flores-Hanson, M.S.E., and Gloria Rosso-White

ABDO Publishing Company

capstone
www.capstoneclassroom.com

Credits
Curriculum Coordinator: Nancy Tuminelly
Cover and Interior Design and Production: Mighty Media
Child Photography: Steven Wewerka, Wewerka Photography
Photo Credits: AbleStock, Anders Hanson, Photodisc

ISBN 978-1-4966-0379-1 (paperback)

Printed in the United States of America.
10908R

SandCastle™ books are created by a professional team of educators, reading specialists, and content developers around five essential components that include phonemic awareness, phonics, vocabulary, text comprehension, and fluency. All books are written, reviewed, and leveled for guided and early intervention reading, and designed for use in shared, guided, and independent reading and writing activities to support a balanced approach to literacy instruction.

SandCastle Level: Beginning

Vv

ABCChDEFGH
IJKLLLMNÑOP
QRSTUVWXYZ

abcchdefgh
ijklllmnñop
qrstuvwxyz

Valeria

Víctor

violín

verduras

ventana

vaso

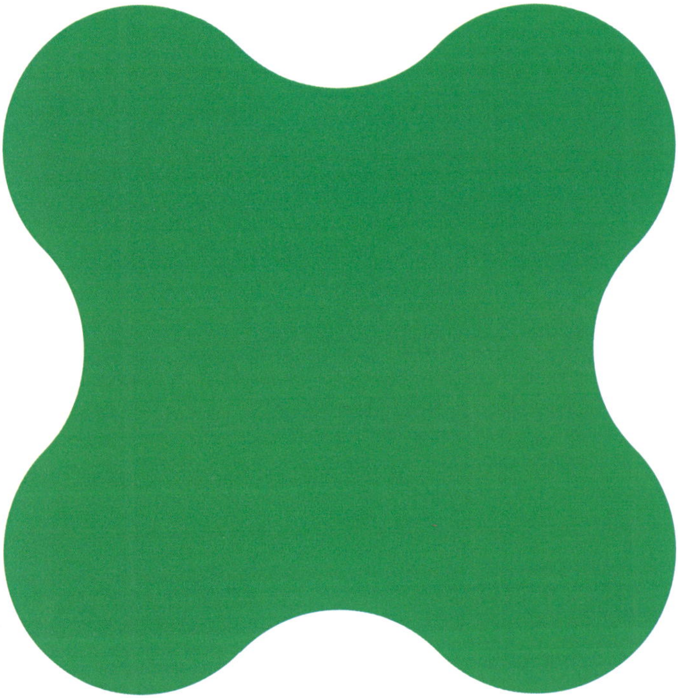

verde

Aquí hay un .

Mira las  .

Veo una .

El  es alto.

El color es .

Valeria tiene una ventana.

La ventana es de madera.

Víctor tiene pintura verde.

La pintura está en la brocha.

A Víctor le gusta
el color verde.

Víctor pinta la
ventana verde.

¿Cuáles de estas cosas comienzan con v?

Más palabras que comienzan con v

vaca

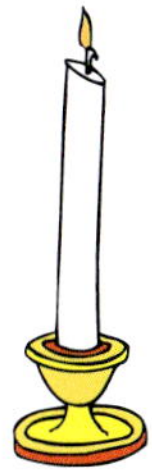

vela

venado

video

violeta

About SandCastle™

A professional team of educators, reading specialists, and content developers created the SandCastle™ series to support young readers as they develop reading skills and strategies and increase their general knowledge. The SandCastle™ series has four levels that correspond to early literacy development in young children. The levels are provided to help teachers and parents select the appropriate books for young readers.

Emerging Readers
(no flags)

Beginning Readers
(1 flag)

Transitional Readers
(2 flags)

Fluent Readers
(3 flags)

These levels are meant only as a guide. All levels are subject to change.

ABDO Publishing Company
www.abdopub.com

capstone
www.capstoneclassroom.com